KT-574-872

out of India

out of India

An Anglo-Indian Childhood

Jamila Gavin

Hodder
Children's
Books

a division of Hodder Headline Limited

Acknowledgements

Thanks to Alan Campbell-Johnson and Robert Hale
Publishers for permission to use the extract from
Mission with Mountbatten on pages 55-56 and 81-83.

This edition published by Hodder Children's Books 2002

Text copyright © Jamila Gavin 1997

First published by Pavilion Books Ltd, London

Book design by Joy Mutter

Cover illustration by Andy Bridge

The right of Jamila Gavin to be identified as the author of the
work has been asserted by her in accordance with the Copyright,
Designs and Patents Act 1988.

10 9 8 7 6 5

A catalogue record for this book is available from the British
Library.

ISBN: 0 340 85462 6

All rights reserved. Apart from any use permitted under UK
copyright law, this publication may only be reproduced, stored or
transmitted, in any form, or by any means with prior permission in
writing of the publishers or in the case of reprographic production
in accordance with the terms of licences issued by the Copyright
Licensing Agency.

Printed by Bookmarque Ltd, Croydon, Surrey
Hodder Children's Books
a division of Hodder Headline Limited
338 Euston Road
London NW1 3BH

For my parents,
to whom I owe everything

Contents

Chapter 1

Boasting

I USED TO BOAST ABOUT many things when I was a child, especially on the occasions that we came over to England from India – three times before I was eleven years old – and each time I had to start making friends all over again in a new school. So when I was asked questions about myself in the different school playgrounds I got to know, it would often go as follows:

Q: '*Where do you come from?*'
A: 'India.'
I knew they thought of tigers and elephants

and monkeys and fakirs sleeping on beds of
nails.

Q: '*Where were you born?*'
A: 'In the Himalayas.'
That impressed them. They imagined my
mother giving birth to me on the icy slopes of
Mount Everest some twenty-nine thousand
feet up, when in fact I was born about six
thousand feet up in the Community Hospital,
Landour, Mussoorie which was in the foothills
of the Himalayas.

Q: '*Did you live in a mud hut?*'
Most people used to think that because
India had so much poverty, everyone lived in a
mud hut. First of all, in real poverty, you
don't live in a mud hut but in a hovel made
up of rags or sticks, or you are a pavement
dweller and have nothing but a scrap of
material. Secondly, mud huts may sound
primitive, but they can be perfect dwelling
places and ecologically, superbly efficient. In

village India, which is where most people still live in such dwellings, they are kept beautifully clean and with a sense of pride. But even if a large number of people live in so-called mud huts – at one time, India was eighty per cent agricultural – there are now hundreds of towns and cities in which people live in homes made of bricks and mortar and stone and glass and concrete. In fact, it is sometimes hard to know if you are in Bombay or Los Angeles.

But me, I boasted:

A: 'I live in a palace.'

This was true – although it wasn't exactly Buckingham Palace. It was a palace designed by an Italian for a Sikh prince, Sher Singh, some two hundred years ago and then abandoned. It was deserted with a huge, wild, overgrown garden with mango and banana trees, and snakes in the grass and a water tank full of frogs and huge high pillars and terraces where wild bees made enormous bee hives which hung like buzzing sacks. I think there must have been pomegranates too, because the palace was called 'Anarkali', meaning pomegranate.

Q: *'Have you ever seen a tiger?'*
I may have been a boaster, but I wasn't a liar, and to this day, I can't say that I have. But I still managed to make it sound glamorous and dangerous.
A: 'Not exactly, but I've seen its footprints in the mud and followed it all along the banks of the Brahmaputra River, and I've seen the long grass crushed where it has just lain, and I've seen the remains of its dinner still fresh, and known that it was not far away – maybe even watching us.'

I have also seen a dead leopard, shot by an American teenager up in the hills. It was the first time I felt sadness at the death of such a beautiful creature, and wasn't too keen on the delight with which he was skinning it – I supposed to put on his wall. But when I was a child in India, people still hunted animals as though there was no end to them. They killed tigers and leopards and cheetahs and deer and birds and butterflies and moths and lizards and spiders and anything that caught their eye. They killed not just for sport, but to collect. As some people collected stamps or coloured sweet papers, they collected dead creatures. I've seen jars of spiked insects; and drawers full of butterflies and walls covered with skins and antlers and heads of deer and tigers gazing out with glassy eyes. The word for a hunter in Urdu is shikari – and in those days everybody hunted.

Seeing how easily I could get a crowd of children round me, enthralled at my tales, I would point to a hole in my school jumper – actually made by a moth – but I would say, 'See this hole? I was shot by a dacoit, a bandit, and this is the bullet hole.' Sometimes, the bullet would become an arrow or a spear.

Did I say I never lied? I lie. I did lie – well, I told stories, as they say! I kind of felt that if it was possible that it could have happened, that was only a step away from it having really happened – and I'd been brought up on hair-raising tales about bandits in India; how they often attacked trains; how cunning they were. They could hide in the lavatories or even under the train seats, then leap out and cut everyone's throats when they were asleep and steal all their belongings. It could have happened to me. But it didn't.

Q: *'Were you born with your red mark in the wrong place?'*
A: 'Don't be daft.'

They had strange ideas, some of these children. On the side of my nose was a red spot, left over from measles. It was there for years, and children often asked if I had been born with my red mark in the wrong place. They were referring to the red bindi which

Indian women wear in the middle of their foreheads and they thought that Indian women were somehow born with it instead of putting it on themselves as other women put on lip-stick or mascara. But I was ignorant myself. I didn't know that a bindi could tell you whether the woman was married or not; if she had been to the temple and a priest had blessed her; which sect she followed: Vishnu or Shiva. So I just laughed at them.

Q: *'Have you ever walked on fire?'*
They had heard stories, not just about the Indian rope trick and holy men sleeping on beds of nails, but of people who walked barefoot across hot coals.

A: 'No, but I have seen all sorts of extraordinary feats, like holy men with nails pierced through their skin or men who could swallow glass and eat fire and contort their bodies into the most unbelievable shapes.' And I saw people who claimed to be levitating – though because it always took place under a blanket,

I was never quite sure whether or not it was a trick!

Q: *'Do you have a bow and arrow?'*
A: 'Of course not.'

Some English children brought up on cowboys and Indians, thought all Indians were American Indians with feathers in their hair. One little boy very considerately gave me a bow and arrows for my sixth birthday. I'm ashamed to this day to remember my rebuff to him. I can hear my sharp high voice saying, 'I never use a bow and arrows,' and casting his gift aside.

I remember one question and answer which brought hoots of laughter from the children. They were talking about which star signs they had been born under, and I proclaimed very boastfully, 'I was born under Leo!' To which someone retorted, quick as a flash, 'I bet Leo had a surprise!'

But I was born under Leo – and I can't help remembering that Leo is the king of the beasts; that August was considered the month of rulers and kings because it was also the sign of the sun. Egyptian Pharaohs and Roman Emperors valued the month of August and tried to have their offspring born then for this reason. To be honest, I don't really believe any of it – and I don't think I'm at all typical of a Leo.

But even though now I don't boast quite as much as I used to, I am still fascinated by the associations there are with the place where I was born, and in what month and year, and what was going on – not just in the mystical world, but in the real world outside. So perhaps my autobiography should start something like this:

I was born in India on 9th August 1941 more than six thousand feet up in the foothills of the Himalayas.

It was a birthplace I was to be very proud of all my life, because the Himalayas were considered by the Hindus to be the dwelling place of the gods. It was a paradise containing the sacred River Ganga which Lord Brahma, the Creator, only allowed to flow to a thirsty earth after much imploring by a king who was granted the lives of his sons if their ashes were mingled with the waters of the River Ganga; it is where Lord Shiva used to sit on icy peaks in long and deep meditation; it is where Lord Indra had his heaven along with his angels and wind warriors, and whose neighbours were Yama, Lord of the Dead, Vayu, God of the Wind and Agni, Lord of Fire. It was the roof of the world.

But when I was born, most of the world was experiencing one of the darkest periods in modern history. Hitler and the Nazis were terrorizing the globe. They had already invaded most of Europe and were now in Russia, heading for Moscow. They were succeeding in the desert under General Rommel, and their dreaded submarines, as ruthless as sharks, had inflicted appalling losses on British battle and merchant ships.

By 7th December, Japan would become a deadly enemy too, attacking the United States fleet at Pearl Harbor, and thus bringing the Americans decisively into the war. That is why it was now truly a World War.

But, for the moment, none of this impinged very much on my mother, father and older brother as they prepared for my arrival. The only battle they were involved in was the battle against nature. It was the height of the monsoon season when, as Hindu mythology states, Lord Indra and his wind warriors, the Maruts, were attacking the Drought Demons with thunder, lightning and torrential rain.

It was through this battle with the elements, struggling down twisting paths which had turned into rushing streams, that on 9th August my mother was carried in a dandy to the Community Hospital, where she gave birth to me at about three in the afternoon. The first thing my older brother Indrajit remarked on being brought to see me was, 'baby has no teeth'.

Chapter 2

Mother, Father, brother and me

B Y BEING SUCH A TERRIBLE BOASTER and telling everyone that I lived in a palace, it somehow suited me to allow my English classmates to believe that because I had lived in a palace, I must be a princess.

But I was no princess. Actually, I was the daughter of an Indian father and an English mother who were both teachers.

My father's family were probably Rajputs, a generation or so back, and would have been from the Kshatriya caste – which is the caste of warriors and princes. However, by becoming a Christian and marrying an English woman, my father lost his caste and, strictly speaking, all of us children are 'untouchables'. So that puts us in our place.

My mother was a child of the potteries in Staffordshire. Her family and relations had rural names like Dean, Lea, Heath and Woods – all pottery names in that area – and they had worked alongside such well-known people as Josiah Wedgwood, Thomas Whieldon and the Johnson brothers. Her father was Meshach Dean – a name which we felt suited his Old Testament severity – and she was Florence Harriet Jessica, known familiarly as 'Jess'.

Both my parents were ambitious and adventurous. Both went to university: my father first in Lahore, then Bristol, and my mother was one of the first young women from her district to get a scholarship to Cambridge. Coming from different ends of the globe, they met in Persia – as Iran was then called – having accepted teaching jobs there

with the Church Missionary Society (CMS).
Against all the norms of the times, they
decided to marry.

Neither seems, however, to have
encountered any hostility from their families.
Well, my father wouldn't because by the time
he married my mother, his parents had both
died, and as the eldest son, he was head of the
family. My mother went back to Staffordshire,
told her parents of her intentions, then got on
a boat to India. My father met her in Bombay
and they were married there in the chapel at
Church Missionary Society House.

My mother now found herself with three
brothers- and six sisters-in-law, but what a
wonderful family they turned out to be – and
how we children loved their names. All our
uncles' names ended in the sound 'ence'. My
father is Terence, followed by his brothers,
Laurence, Endurance and Valence. My aunts'
names all ended in the sound 'een': Loreen,
Maureen, Irene, Emreen, Catherine and

Shireen.

Because the family were Christian, they had taken on a Christian surname, 'Phillips', as was customary when an Indian converted to Christianity. These surnames were usually biblical and in my family's case the name was also historic. They say that my great-great-grandfather saved a British officer called Phillips during one of the uprisings which would lead, eventually, to independence for India. The British officer rewarded him for his pains by converting him to Christianity and giving him his name. I still feel it is one of my tasks in life to track down the records of this conversion, and find out more about it. However, because my father identified so strongly with Indian nationalism and the drive for independence, he changed his name back to the old Indian family name, Khushal-Singh, though he is, to this day, a committed Christian.

So our lives were never going to fit into any kind of stereotype. We were not brought up as

Indians following Hindu, Sikh or Muslim
practices, nor were we English. Indeed, we
were probably regarded by many with great
distaste, being neither one thing nor the other.
We weren't even genuine Anglo-Indians, for it
was carefully pointed out to me only recently,
that you had to have had an English father
and an Indian mother to count as an Anglo-
Indian. Apparently I could describe myself as
Eurasian! So long as I can call myself a
human being, I don't mind.

But I don't remember ever having any crisis
of identity or culture. My parents' belief in
their own values was too strong and we
children inherited that. They believed in the
universal ideals of Christianity and Gandhism;
the brotherhood of man and democracy. Our
names reflected their belief in tolerance: my
name Jamila (Muslim) Elizabeth (Christian)
Khushal-Singh (Hindu/Sikh) was a mix of
several beliefs; my brother was Indrajit Philip.
Though we were brought up in the Church of
England, it was with a great sense of respect

that we lived side by side with Hindus, Muslims, Sikhs, Parsees and all manner of Christian sects.

If there is anything I regret, it is that we were brought up quite so 'western'; in the sense that we lived according to western life styles, in a western-style bungalow, speaking English, wearing western clothes and going to church on Sundays. I knew more about Beethoven sonatas than Indian ragas and I never properly learned an Indian language. However, that did not make my parents mere puppets of the Empire. My father was a passionate nationalist and follower of Gandhi. So keen a disciple was he, that he wore homespun cotton cloth called khadi and sat cross-legged on the floor each day to do some spinning – this was Gandhi's way of identifying himself with the poorest of the land down to the 'untouchables'. Gandhi took his identification to such lengths that not only did he travel third class on the train with the peasants, eat the simplest diet of yoghurt, milk, fruit and nuts, but he didn't compromise his stand for anyone. Even in England, when he had an audience with the king, he appeared looking as emaciated as a beggar in his simple one-piece homespun cotton dhoti and sandalled feet. Apparently the king asked him, 'And how is India, Mr Gandhi?' to which Gandhi reputedly replied, 'as you see me, Your Highness'.

Gandhi's simple but arrow-straight logic was intensely appealing. His extraordinary powers of communication and persuasion enabled him to get the politicians to adopt 'Satyaghara' – non-violent action – as the means to achieving independence from Britain. He renamed the 'untouchables' the 'Harijans', which means the children of God, and made it illegal for them to be discriminated against. His ideas went far beyond theory and philosophy; they were as comprehensive as a religion, embodying all aspects of his daily life. My father went to his ashram to learn from Gandhi himself.

Earlier, Gandhi had created a 'Tolstoy Farm' based on the Russian novelist, Leo Tolstoy's theories of education: that we should all learn as a family; that education was not just learning to read and write in isolation, but must be a part of every-day living; that teachers must be prepared to do anything they asked their children to do; that everyone should learn to spin cotton as a symbol of the need for self-sufficiency; that there should be no servants, and no job was too menial for anyone to undertake; and, believing in non-violence as he did, there was no corporal punishment at his school, but only the power of reason, which I think even Gandhi could find taxing at times! Children not only learned several Indian languages, but Gandhi also believed in the equal importance of physical and spiritual training. Other such schools were being founded in Britain, like A. S. Neil's school Summerhill and the Elmhirsts' community, farm and school at Dartington.

Alas, my father let us down on the language side. Why, oh why, did he not ensure we learned the beautiful Urdu he spoke?

Later, my father threw himself more actively into the cause of Indian independence and we were brought up with the names of not only Gandhi, but Nehru, Sir Stafford Cripps, Mountbatten and, of course, the founder of Pakistan, Muhammad Ali Jinnah.

My mother was embedded in her English education with a great knowledge and love of literature, history and philosophy and this she imparted wholeheartedly to us. I think one of my earliest memories has to be of my mother playing the piano – probably Beethoven, as her father had been an amateur pianist with a particular passion for this composer (to this day, I have his copy of the Beethoven sonatas with my grandfather's ticks and metronome markings). She also played Mozart and Schubert, whose music was as familiar to us as eating and drinking. We delighted in hearing how she went to a vast warehouse in

Lahore, which was then a part of India, and chose a piano out of the many hundreds of pianos which had been brought in and then abandoned by the British. Having picked her piano, it was then loaded onto a bullock cart and trundled several miles to Narowal, and then a second time, when we all moved to Batala. Jingle jangle must have been the sound it made as it was loaded and unloaded.

Batala was the small town in the Punjab we all moved to after I was born. My father was sent to be headmaster of a little Christian school there. The school had been founded a hundred years earlier by Miss Maria Tucker and her friend and colleague, Francis Baring of the famous Baring family, who were bankers and governors. In good Empire spirit, they longed to bring Christian education to the 'heathens'. Maria Tucker must have been a remarkable woman, and much admired by the local people, for they always referred to her as A Lady of England – ALOE – a term which has lasted to this day almost like CBE

or OBE. And on her grave in the nearby
churchyard is inscribed 'Maria Charlotte
Tucker, ALOE'. The little school which she
founded was called the Baring School, but
more popularly referred to as the ALOE
school.

Nearby was a huge, crumbling mansion of
many terraces and verandahs, painted with
fading murals and ornamented with intricate
mouldings. The building had been designed
and built by an Italian architect in about 1855
for Prince Sher Singh, son of Ranjit Singh, one
of the great rulers of the Punjab. It was within
the grounds of an already existing estate
dating from the fifteenth century. This was the
palace of which I was to boast. We moved in
and inhabited its lovely spacious rooms, with
its tall, elegant windows looking out from
every side, and the remarkable drawing room
which was described as the most beautiful in
north India – we inherited much of the
furniture which had been specially designed
for it!

I had a whole nursery all to myself.

So here we lived for the next six years of my life. Six idyllic years for a child, but a nightmare for others in that period.

While I was learning to walk, to run, to ride a bike, to swim, to steal sugar cane and suck mangoes, children in other parts of the world were being bombed, orphaned, displaced and separated from their parents. I couldn't imagine how they could stand it. I was immensely attached to my mother, and felt panic-stricken at the thought of ever being separated from her for any reason whatsoever. Nor was I ever separated from her for any length of time, though for some reason, my brother went to boarding schools in the hills at quite an early age and claimed to love it.

I envied my brother. He seemed to have the freedom and independence that I craved. He would go roaming with his pals, and I know I was always begging to be allowed to tag along. But I was despised for being a girl, and only really played with him when he had no one else. Then his games were relentless and exhausting. Long after I had tired of hide-and-seek or guli dunda (a kind of Indian rounders), he was ready to go on and on and on, and would get furious with me for giving up. Maybe it was to keep up with my brother, and earn his respect, that I was game for anything. If he climbed trees and explored abandoned houses and jumped across difficult ditches or went adventuring, I did too. He could swim before I could – well, he was three years older than me. Once, when he was swimming in the tank, I just jumped in too and promptly sank to the bottom because I hadn't yet learned. I can remember his shout of alarm as he and my father dashed to pull me out.

Even now as adults, we find ourselves daring each other. Not so long ago, when he visited me in England, my friends were appalled when we both competitively eyed up a fallen branch which had formed a bridge high across a muddy stream. It would take balance and judgement to walk it, and a nasty tumble if we fell in. But because he did it, I had to – and did.

I didn't really play with dolls. In fact, such toys weren't available in India when I was a child. Whatever dolls I had were brought from England, and many of my early ones were made of pottery, and therefore breakable. I was obviously an incredibly clumsy mother with my pottery babies, because I was always breaking them. Then the day came when I was given the latest sensation – an 'UNBREAKABLE DOLL'. It must have been made of plastic or some such material. Here I was, boasting about my unbreakable doll, when my brother, a born scientist, said, 'let's test it out'. So he took my doll (with me protesting loudly, as I recall), and we both climbed to the highest terrace of the palace – so high that you could see the Himalayas in the distance, and the countryside stretching away for miles. There he held my doll over the balustrade and we gazed down, down to the stone terrace far below. I know I didn't want him to do it, but he had already challenged me. 'It's supposed to be unbreakable, isn't it? So what are you worrying about?' Then he let go. Poor dolly (which had not yet been given a name); it might have been unbreakable in my clumsy handling at ground level, but it could not survive a plunge of seventy or more feet down onto the stone verandah.

I don't recall my brother really getting told off. Well, how could he? He was always so logical – and still is. A kind of Mr Spock! He did the same to my mother's wireless in England. He took the whole thing to bits and spread it out on the living room carpet. My mother was horrified. But this time, he was able to put it all back together again. And it worked.

With all my boasting, I never bothered to mention all the other different kinds of homes we lived in after the palace. Nothing ever seemed as interesting again. The palace was converted to a College of Higher Education, to be known as Baring Christian College, and because it was my father who initiated the college and became its first principal, I was the first principal's daughter. Fifty odd years later, on returning there, I was still introduced as 'the First Principal's Daughter'.

But now that the palace had become a college full of teachers and pupils, we had to move to a typical mission bungalow down the road. It was made of brick with white plastered walls and had a stone verandah all the way round. I remember a long cool living room, with blinds and curtains which flapped lazily. I remember low tables with vases and bowls – and in particular a rich Venetian blue glass fruit dish, whose elegance and beauty stays in my memory to this day.

As with most British-built bungalows, we had no inner courtyards like many traditional Indian homes. All the rooms led from one to another, but each was separated by either a door or a curtain, and with its own entrance

27

from a point on the verandah. The bathroom
was at the back. It was an Indian-style
bathroom – a stone, windowless room, with
just an enclosed stone space on the floor with
a low surround like a wall on which you
could put a mug or a soap dish. There was
one tap, a plug, as well as the essential jug
and bucket. I think there was also a tin bath
which I probably was bathed in as a baby. To
have a hot bath, the water had to be heated in
the kitchen which was outside where our cook
lived. The cook would heat the water on an
open fire in a large saucepan; the bearer
would carry the water; and the ayah would
bathe us. Because of caste, it was inconceiv-
able that either would do anyone else's job –
though my parents would do anything as and
when it was necessary.

The image of water is strong. I see water
held in the cup of the hand to drink, to rinse
your mouth after teeth brushing and to wash
the face and the arms. I see a long cataract of
silver liquid pouring steadily and economically

from a jug – over the body and over the head.
I see brown skin glistening with water. I see
water belching out from the pump and the
spray of water like tossed diamonds flung out
of the watering can onto the dry flower beds.
I see water glinting dark and dangerous at the
bottom of a forty-foot-deep well. I see water
spewed out from a carousel of tin cans,
tossing it out into gulleys to irrigate the fields
as the bullock or camel or buffalo treads its
path round and round the well, and I see rain
water sheeting down during monsoon, and
people rushing out with open mouths and
outstretched arms, their clothes merging into
their skins. Water is precious. Water is sacred.

Spiders love water too. The image of spiders
is strong. As in England, spiders love
bathrooms. It must be the cool and water
which attracts them – but I'm sorry to say, I
hated them and screamed as if I was being
murdered at the sight of one. People often
wondered why, when I was born in India,
wasn't I used to it? How could I make so

much fuss about spiders and creepy crawlies? Well, I just did. Indian spiders are so big and hairy and scuttley, and as for cockroaches – UGH! When I grew up, I kind of got over spiders. I don't scream any more, and certainly never kill them, but cockroaches still make me shudder down to my toes. Perhaps I learned this aversion from my mother. I see her sitting in one of those cane chairs on the verandah with her feet up, having an afternoon cup of tea, when from out of the cane came a large, brown crackly cockroach. I didn't see it till it was perched on her shoulder. Then I screamed AAAAHHH!

'What?' cried my mother. 'What's the matter?'

'There's a cockroach on you!' I yelled.

'AAAAHHH!' screamed my mother, leaping up and spilling her tea. 'Where?'

'On your shoulder!' I gasped, and then watched with a mixture of horror and amusement as she struck at herself madly to flick it off.

But to go back to houses. The lavatory in

Batala was actually a wooden commode. We used to call it the throne. Some could be quite high, which you reached by climbing a step. You sat there, did your business, then climbed down shutting the lid after you. It was then the job of the sweeper – who of course was of the 'untouchable' caste – to come and empty it at the end of the day, by which time there was a terrible smell. Don't ask me where she emptied it – I don't know. But, oh how I remember the day my father had a flush lavatory installed. To have a flush lavatory seemed to be the last word in luxury. It had a china bowl and a wooden lid; a long metal drainpipe went up to a metal cistern from which hung a long metal chain with a wooden handle on the end of it. I had to jump to reach the chain. The flush of rushing water excited and terrified me. I was sure a beastie lived in the lavatory bowl and that by flushing, it would leap out and gobble me up. So I used to pull the chain, then run screaming from the bathroom all the way through the dark intervening rooms to the living room. But it was a huge improvement on the throne.

The kitchen was in an outhouse. All it consisted of was a clay oven and possibly a paraffin stove, with various utensils such as a grinding stone to grind the spices, a bowl for mixing chapatti flour, a board for rolling out the dough, various containers for cooking rice and vegetables, and a water pitcher. It was all such fun. I was always hanging around our cook, a man called Ujaga, and helping roll out the chapattis. From that modest place came dishes fit for a rajah. It was never the same in an English kitchen.

After eating, the dishes would be washed up Indian style, which is to first scour them with ashes or dry earth, then to rinse them out under the pump – not by the cook, of course, but perhaps by a young girl or boy from the village. As for the pump, I adored flying up and down on the end of the handle, and it hardly mattered if you got wet, for under the Indian sun, you dried in seconds.

Chapter 3

First voyage

IN 1944, WHEN I WAS THREE years old, there was a lull in the war. Everyone thought the war was over, and P&O Liners decided to send a passenger ship back to England. There were many English people like my mother, longing to see their homes and relatives who had suffered greatly through the Blitz. My mother decided to go with me and my brother. I have so many jumbled memories of journeys in India: of being picked up in my father's arms, being propped on the cross-bar of bicycles; memories of bullock carts and tonga rides with luggage, and crowded railway stations and battling for seats; and sleeping in the roof rack during the two nights and three days it took the train to get from Batala in the Punjab, to Bombay way down towards the south.

They were cautious on the boat. We each were given a life jacket and had life-boat drill standing in lines every morning on deck – just in case there was a lurking German U-boat, ready to blast us out of the water. We were accompanied by a flotilla of battle ships to protect us and I remember once, a sea plane landed alongside us. The long gangway was lowered, and some personage was transferred from the plane via a small dingy to the gang plank and brought on board our ship. It was all very exciting which is why, I'm sure, I remember it all. I can remember the feel and smell of the life jacket and the way we had to tie it round our chests. I fell in love with life on board – and the sailors. I swore that when I grew up I would marry a captain and go to sea with him!

England was a shock. Like Dick
Whittington, I suppose I expected the streets
to be paved with gold. Buckingham Palace
was a bitter shock – it didn't look anything
like the pictures in my fairy-tale books of
castles with tall turrets, and gold flecked
sloping roofs, and balconies and ramparts
from which beautiful queens waved their
handkerchiefs at departing knights as they
went into battle. This was the capital of the
Empire: this was the most powerful country in
the world and I thought it would be a
glittering, magnificent place, but it wasn't and
I was quite disgusted. The London I saw was
so grey and bleak and drab – and when the
winter came, so cold. I suffered terribly from
chilblains on my toes and heels – and the tops
of my hands were chapped till they bled. I
remember the puff of gas stoves being lit.
They were divided into three sections, and for
economy's sake, you could light one or two
sections; three if you felt hugely extravagant.
But they only seemed to heat one bit of you at

a time. Gas was the most common fuel. Even
many of the lights in the flat in which we
stayed were gaslights. My mother had to build
tall towers of sixpences and shillings to feed
the gas metre.

We took a steam train from London to my
grandfather's home in Newcastle-under-Lyme.
Now this was a house such as I had seen in
English books, but never lived in, so I found it
interesting. It had all the rooms a house
should have: a downstairs living room, a
parlour, a kitchen, and best of all, an upstairs.
Stairs were so exciting because Indian
bungalows don't have stairs and Indian
houses, if they have upper floors or balconies,
are reached by stone steps going up the
outside, so we tended to pound up and down
grandfather's stairs till he got quite annoyed.
Upstairs were three bedrooms. I don't recall a
bathroom. I suppose it had an inside lavatory,
but I don't remember it. The front room,
which was the living room, was generally kept
closed except when visitors came, so it was

always tidy and neat, but freezing cold. The back room was where everyone really lived. It had sofas and chairs and a fire burning all the time and a tiled fireplace with brass animals inside the fender, and a toasting fork where we could toast buns for tea. It was the only room that was warm. Even the kitchen was only warm when there was cooking going on.

Having a bath was, for me, standing up in the sink, while my mother douched me down. It was a chilly affair – no fun at all. I don't remember my bedroom. But I do recall having to sleep with my Aunty Rene once, when we visited her. (She wasn't really my aunt, but my mother's best friend, and I hated her. She smelt of lavender and wore mauve – a colour I have loathed ever since. I don't know why I hated her. I don't remember her being unkind to me. She used to give me a boiled egg in an egg cup and chopped my toast up into soldiers. But I just hated her powdery smell of lavender.) When we visited other friends of my mother or relatives out in the country, they had lavatories outside, or at the bottom of the garden. Going to the toilet was sheer torture in England – inside the house or out – as was having a bath.

At that time, it seemed to me that all gardens in England tended to smell of dank, wet cabbages. I suppose it was part of 'Digging for Victory', when everyone was encouraged to grow as much food as possible because of Hitler's food blockades. He intended to starve the British into surrender. But I do remember a vast back garden in Shepherd's Bush where we once had a flat, which had iron steps descending into a dense jungle of brambles and weeds and climbing roses. I would stand at the top and look down, awestruck by the power of nature as soon as man turned his back.

I never knew my paternal grandparents because they died before my parents even married, so I hang on to what memories I have of my maternal grandparents.

My grandfather frightened me. He was

enormously strict and very serious, with
round, stern blue eyes. I don't remember him
ever smiling, or ever treating me with any
kindness. I just knew that my mother admired
him tremendously – he was so well read and
knowledgeable. She always said he could have
been anything he wanted: a doctor, a
professor or a musician; he not only loved
music but tuned his own piano. He was
meticulous about everything he did. He would
correct me all the time: 'Sit up straight. Don't
slouch. Read with the light over your left
shoulder. Chew your food twenty times.' If he
went for a walk, he walked behind us with his
cane. He told me that I rolled one of my feet
out when I walked, and he would rap my
ankle with his cane to remind me to turn it
inwards. When we sat at table for meals, he
himself would tuck me up to the table. There
were no high chairs, so I was seated on a
cushion, but the table still came up to my
chin. Then be would tuck a vast napkin into
his chest, take up the mcat knife and the

sharpener and swipe the two implements together, looking as though he was going to carve me up instead of the beef. How different from India and the soft-footed bearer who would pad in from the kitchen with dishes piled high with the whitest of white fragrant rice, and steaming tureens of delectable mutton curry and spicy potatoes and the wonderful plate of newly made chapattis, wrapped in white napkins. For me, English food was epitomized by the smell of over-boiled cabbage.

Grandmother was gentle, kind, silent, nearly blind and partly paralysed after a stroke, and that is all I know of her. The photograph I have of her as a young woman shows that she was beautiful. I sense that she was patient, loyal, non-combative and sad.

After visiting the grandparents, back we went to London.

The city was battered and bombed. The bomb sites were awful but exciting: full of

Michaelmas daisies and nettles and ragwort and bay willow herb – and ankle-breaking rubble and dangerous walls which hadn't fallen down, and exposed staircases and rooms in which you could see the wallpaper and the fireplaces; and there were vast holes in the ground where houses had simply disappeared.

The dark alleys round the churches seemed to attract blackberries at the end of the summer, and I will always remember the enjoyment, and the sense of survival I got when I staunched my appetite by eating these blackberries – or the leaves of the hawthorn which we called bread and cheese. I was even known to crunch on an acorn from time to time on the grounds that if pigs could eat them, why not me? I suppose it's a wonder I wasn't poisoned.

The war wasn't over. By no means. We had no sooner arrived and gone to stay with my Aunty Molly in Streatham, than the Nazis started bombing again. I know I was only three, but I'm not lying when I say I remember the siren going off, and all of us draped in blankets with pillow in hand, trooping out into the garden to descend into the Anderson shelter during an air raid. When we came out, all the windows in my aunt's flat had been blown in. A house down the road got the full blast.

The Germans had invented the doodlebug. This was an unmanned bomb with a beeper in it which came buzz, buzz, buzz over the city. People would stop and stare in horror. They would be listening. So long as the beeper was buzzing, the bomb was airborne and on the move. It was when the beeping stopped that you knew it was over its target. Everyone tried to gauge where it would stop and into which street or building it would plunge. But what could you do, except rush out of the house and watch it do its worst?

Aunty Mollie had a first floor flat, high ceilinged and large, in a typical London house built at the turn of the century, but now converted into numerous flats. I slept in one bed with my cousin Patricia – end to end.

I loved my Aunty Mollie. If I ever lost my mother, Aunty Mollie would have been my mother substitute. She had the kindest face, with slightly sloping eyes like the eyes of a bloodhound (but that's where the resemblance ends). She was very pretty, I thought, as beautiful as my mother, and always dressed stylishly, even though it was hard to look anything but drab in wartime Britain.

Patricia was beautiful too, in an Anglo-Saxon way. She had a lovely face, with a peaches-and-cream skin, a neat slim nose, wide blue eyes and magnificent long golden hair which hung straight and glistening like a waterfall. And she was nice – really nice. She tried to teach me to skip, but I couldn't jump over the rope and get it over my head, so I just wriggled it in front of me, jumped up and down and cried, 'Look at me skipping!' Patricia would have been about seven years old, but I never thought of her as a child, more a beautiful lady – she seemed so grown up.

I know I remember the sirens and the sound of bombers going overhead in formation, low and heavy with bombs. They were sounds so embedded, and brought such terror, that I was amazed when, after the war, factories used a similar siren to herald the start and end of the shift. I wondered why it didn't instil panic in people. Often a motorbike can make a note as it goes through a neighbourhood that is at exactly the same pitch as those bomber planes flying in formation. Until I was about ten or eleven years old, I would duck under the bedclothes at that sound.

So, my mother took us back to India again. How she knew of a boat that was going and managed to get us tickets, I really don't know. We travelled to the port by train, with blackedout windows so that the Nazi bombers wouldn't see us.

I remember happier train journeys in England; there were many. There's me gazing at my reflection and watching beads of rain shuddering and sliding both downwards and

upwards on the window panes; the shriek of
the train whistle and the black soot spewing
out into the air in the long trail of smoke.

I was so thrilled by the speed and the clatter
and the stations whizzing by. I remember
leaning out of the window waving madly at
the guard, as our train pulled out of yet
another station from somewhere to
somewhere. One of my favourite poems which
I feel I knew from at least that time was the
one by Robert Louis Stevenson:

Faster than fairies, faster than witches,
Bridges and houses, hedges and ditches;
And charging along like troops in a battle,
All through the meadows the horses and
cattle;
All of the sights of the hill and the plain
Fly as thick as driving rain;
And ever again, in the wink of an eye,
Painted stations whistle by.

> *'From a Railway Carriage'*
> *A Child's Garden of Verses*

All in the rhythm of the train wheels: de de de dum, de de de dum, de de de dum. It would rattle through my head as the train pounded along.

Apparently we went all the way up to Leith in Scotland.

There we boarded a Polish ship called the Batory. It took us all round the coast of Africa back to India, as it was too dangerous to go through the Mediterranean and the Suez Canal. It was on the Batory we celebrated Christmas and I got measles. I remember staring at my reddened, blotchy face in the mirror next to my upper bunk bed. That was when I got my red mark 'in the wrong place'. Most of the children on that ship went down with measles. Was it on that ship that we children were entertained by Magic Lantern shows? I remember a strange man lying on his back asleep, his mouth slightly open as he snored; a constant line of mice trooped in through his open mouth and out of his nose or ears.

We arrived safely back in Bombay, though later we heard that the captain of the Batory had been arrested for some wartime misdemeanour.

Many years later, when I was about fourteen, and back in England, my class at school did a project on the Port of London Authority – yes, the docks then were still a viable working industry right in the heart of London. We were taken on a cruise down the Thames, having all the sights of London pointed out to us, as well as learning about the working of the Port and all the trade which went on; when looming ahead was a huge, rusty old ship anchored by a great long chain. Visible on its prow was the name *Batory*.

Chapter 4

The beginning of the end of an empire

S O WHERE ARE WE NOW? It is 1945 and I am four years old. Anne Frank, who was fourteen, had been discovered by the Nazis hiding in the secret room in Amsterdam and, with her family, sent to Auschwitz and to her death. From its outpost in India, the British had watched in horror as the Japanese conquered everything the British had thought they controlled – from Malaya, Singapore and Burma right up to the borders of India. My mother remembers long convoys of lorries trundling through the night past our

bungalow in Batala, carrying the military up
to the borders in preparation for the Japanese
invasion. What would we have done then?
Where would we have gone? But the invasion
never happened. America and her allies
decided to drop the first nuclear bomb on two
cities in Japan: Hiroshima, on 6th August
and, on my birthday, 9th August, they
dropped the second nuclear bomb on the city
of Nagasaki. For me, it continues to be a
horrible anniversary.

I am sure my parents were aware, at that
time, of the coming to a head of Indian
demands for independence.

There had always been a Hindu prophesy
that the British would leave India within two
hundred years – not that the British believed
any such thing. India was, after all, the jewel
in the crown of a British Empire 'upon which
the sun would never set'. But it was long
instilled in the Indian psyche that the British
would go – must go.

I remember political processions marching

down the road past our bungalow, with
banners and leaders yelling 'Hindustan
Zindabad!', 'Long live India!' But, as the war
finally came to an end and a post-war Labour
Government committed itself to Indian independence, a further movement, spearheaded
by the Muslim leader Muhammad Ali Jinnah,
had now taken hold of India. Jinnah was
described as a severe, unsmiling, gaunt,
brilliant man; trained in Britain as a lawyer, as
Gandhi had been. Jinnah was sure that once
the British left, a predominantly Hindu India
would discriminate against its minority
Muslim population. So he pressed ardently for
a separate country for the Muslims. It was a
bitter blow for Gandhi in particular, whose
whole philosophy was based on the
brotherhood of man, and who, while
recognizing the innate bitterness between
Hindus and Muslims, had been prepared to
sacrifice his life to bring reconciliation
between them. We heard of long walks on
Malabar Hill above Bombay, where Gandhi

pleaded with Jinnah not to separate; where
Nehru was even prepared to give the future
premiership to Jinnah if only India could be
kept together. But all the while, the movement
grew in popularity among the Muslims, and
often the processions passing our bungalow
yelled, 'Pakistan Zindabad!'

Where we lived in the Punjab, we were right
on the dividing line of the proposed partition
of India. There was an added complication.
The Punjab was not just a mixed population
of Hindus and Muslims, it was the traditional
kingdom of the Sikhs and their most sacred
city, Amritsar, was just a few miles away.
Would anyone take notice of their identity,
religion and culture? It was in the interests of
some politicians to put all factions at each
others' throats.

My mother had been expecting her third
child. I remember her pregnant; helping her
with tasks that she began to find difficult. My
second brother, Sushil John, was born on 21st
December 1945. When she came home with

this little baby, I was intensely interested in it. So many people brought him presents. I remember in particular a wooden hockey stick and wooden ball, for the Punjabis were passionate about hockey!

There were worries though. Sushil wasn't well. He was vomiting after feeds. There were visits from the doctor, then he was taken into hospital. There are gaps in my memories. I wasn't a part of the anxiety my parents must have felt. All I remember was a trip to the hospital in a tonga on New Year's Day 1946, and being shown into a small room where a doctor told us that Sushil was dead. I remember my mother and father weeping.

For myself, I didn't understand death. We all looked at his tiny body and I can hear my voice exclaiming, 'Why is baby blue?' Death seemed to mean that Sushil would no longer open his eyes; no longer need to pee; no longer eat or drink; no longer cry. I questioned my father over and over again, trying to understand the difference between being alive and being dead. How painful it must have been for him to reply.

Sushil John was buried with his hockey stick and ball in a grave right next to Maria Charlotte Tucker ALOE.

The epitaph on his grave is as follows:

Urdu:
Yeh gui apri latafad ki dad
Par na saka
Khila to zarur magar
Khilke muskara na saka

English:
This flower did blossom
But could not thrive
It opened, yes,
But could not smile

As the politicians began to look at the map to see where the partition lines should be drawn between India and Pakistan, inter-communal rioting was breaking out all over

India, but especially from Bombay to Calcutta and Delhi to Amritsar. It overflowed with unbelievable ferocity, stemmed by an anguished Gandhi threatening to fast to the death if they didn't stop. My mother, pregnant again, wanted to remove us from the danger area and take me and my brother back to England. My father agreed for us, but he himself was determined to stay put. My mother always used to say he had the luck of the devil. Somehow, he dodged death at every turn, for undoubtedly he was in the very eye of the storm.

As it became impossible to keep open the college, he turned it into a refugee centre and devoted the rest of that dreadful period into organizing food and shelter for the hundreds and thousands of pathetic and traumatized refugees passing in both directions: Muslims to the new Pakistan, and Hindus to be part of India. He also drove truckfuls of the most vulnerable refugees through the ethnically sensitive areas, often having to argue for their lives as well as his own. Well, as my mother always used to say, 'Your father has the gift of the gab!'

At this point I should quote Alan Campbell-Johnson, who was Earl Mountbatten's press attaché leading up to Independence, and who kept a daily diary. He describes Gandhi in a period which veered from the ecstatic and most hopeful, to the depths of evil, cruelty and man's inhumanity to man, and explains how Gandhi was prepared, over and over again, to fast to the death to force enemies to sit down and talk with each other, rather than fight:

> *You have to live in the vicinity of a Gandhi fast to understand its pulling power. The whole of Gandhi's life is a fascinating study in the art of influencing the masses, and judging by the success he has achieved in this mysterious domain, he must be accounted one of the greatest artists in leadership of all time. He has a genius for*

acting through symbols which all can understand. Fasting as a means of moral pressure and purification is part of the fabric of Hindu life. There is the unmistakable sense of everyone being drawn out of this preoccupation to share in a painful responsibility which no man can wholly ignore.

My father couldn't ignore it. I know he could never have walked away from the pain and horror which had come into our lives, destroying all the ideals he held most dear. He was influenced by Gandhi's example, and I still have his many tiny photographs of endless scenes of refugee camps. Edwina, Lady Mountbatten, wife of the Viceroy, Lord Louis Mountbatten, was also deeply involved. She took on arduous programmes of visiting hospitals, clinics, slums, wretched dwellings in cities and villages, and moving heaven and earth to bring succour to vast numbers of dispossessed people surging between the new

Me, as a baby, with my parents and brother

My father, before he met my mother

My mother as a young woman,
after leaving Cambridge

Me, aged 5

My brother and I with baby Rosemary!

St Saviour's Primary School class photo. I'm sixth from the right in the back row

Me, teaching my sister a piano duet

Above: Last day of school. Hooray! 1956
Below: Me, aged 16

divide of India and Pakistan. She came to Batala during one of her many tours and offered my father her support and encouragement. I'm boasting again, but my father was a remarkable man and gave of himself without reserve. And he, like many others, never forgot Lady Mountbatten's charisma and genuine love of India.

Chapter 5

The Second
Voyage to England

MORE TRAVEL; TONGAS, trains,
busy Indian railway stations;
more excitement.

An Indian railway platform is a composite
of all life in India: animal and human. As you
stand there waiting, at any time of night or
day, for a train which could be hours late, the
vendors are cooking any number of delicious
dishes. Everywhere are groups of people or
families, crouched in intimate circles, or
wrapped in shroud-like coverings, grabbing
sleep whenever possible. And watching,

scurrying, poised, coveting, are the rats and cockroaches and ants and dogs and crows and monkeys, all waiting to pounce on any morsel which falls their way. Sometimes, they take things into their own hands – or claws! Once, when the train had pulled into a station, I got off to go and buy a dry banana leaf of vegetable curry from a platform vendor. Little did I know what other eyes were on my food. As I returned with the banana leaf cupped in my hands, a huge crow flew down. It grabbed the edge of the leaf in its beak and pulled it from my hands. All my curry went down on to the platform as the crow flew away. But there wasn't a mess for long. Immediately, the hungry station dogs leapt forward, as did the monkeys, cockroaches and all kinds of other creatures, to consume my meal. As for me, I was forced to go back and start all over again.

We reached Bombay and stayed for a few days in the CMS House there. It was a large red-brick building with two tiers or wire-netted verandahs running all the way round – rather in the style of a tea-planter's house. Bombay was a huge, bustling city that seemed to contain some that was good and much that was bad of humanity. It was in Bombay that I saw sights which would stay with me for ever: skeletal people propped up against walls in the last stages of starvation; limbless beggars propelling themselves along on make-shift wheels; mutilated children whining for alms; pathetic mothers with shrivelled babies at their flat chests – and the grizzled, the blind, bent, disregarded old people. It was then that I first tried to imagine what such people think. What thoughts were in their heads? How did they see us? Did anything make them happy? I saw cruelty, which I couldn't understand. Those thin, bony horses dragging loads far too big, being whipped till they fell. Why? And dogs, the lowest of the low, scavenging, starving, kicked and abused.

But people did it to people too. For every horse with its ribs sticking out, pulling an unbelievable load, was a rickshaw wallah, pulling a bicycle with two families packed into the back, quite unmoved by his muscles straining till they nearly ripped, and the sweat pouring down his neck as, with bent head, he strove to move along through the traffic. For every starving dog was a starving human being. Was this simply what Hindus call karma – fate? The acceptance of your lot? That you live this life in whatever way you can, in order to inherit a better life the next time round? I have pondered this over a lifetime, being beguiled by the philosophy and repelled by the realities in turn. I retain, though, the image of a tiny, thin, ragged beggar girl, carefully carrying in both hands a saucer of milk, steadfastly crossing a busy street, with bicycles and lorries and rickshaws swerving round her, and setting it down before a scraggy, starving, mewling little kitten, and seeing the contentment on her face as she stood back with hand on hip and watched it lap.

There was always excitement. India is dangerous, beautiful, cruel, serene and always exciting. Perhaps I, too, have the luck of the devil. I was always slipping away and having adventures. Like the beggar girl, I was an expert jay-walker – well, it's something you have to develop pretty quickly in a country like India, if you are ever to get across a city road. It is anarchic and chaotic; the sense of each creature for itself. We swung about through the city as monkeys through a jungle; swinging from buses, hanging out of trains and leaping onto the backs of bullock carts, wobbling about on bicycles. So you can imagine how hard it was to come to ordered, law-abiding England. But I didn't project into the future or dread us going back there.

The voyage was thrilling. Once more, the great sea would be our companion; staring for hours through the rails on deck at this vast mass of moving, heaving, swirling, constantly changing creature which did indeed seem to have life. And there were the stops on the way: Port Said, Aden and Gibraltar with all their exotic life. I see dozens of boats rowing eagerly towards our giant ship. Ropes tossed up and fastened, so that baskets with all sorts of wonderful things to buy could be hoisted up and our decks turned into a magic bazaar.

I seemed to find so much to interest me that I was oblivious to any snubs or snobs that were on the ship. My mother experienced it though. She used to say there was an invisible line travelling either way, up to which other children (English children) played with me, but once the line was crossed they fell away and the barriers went up and I played alone.

Perhaps this is why, in order to hang on to some kind of magic, I believed in fairies when I came to England. I needed an inner world which took me out of that grey, drab post-war life which I found grim and punitive. Teachers were severe. Children were not treated with respect. In England, I was cuffed and strapped and whacked in a way I never, never was in India. I developed my phobia for school, and although I displayed an early capriciousness for learning, landed up being innumerate, with a strong aversion to figures for which I was then punished throughout the rest of my school life. Luckily, I not only had learned to read before I went to school, but my love of books and stories was so strong, not even school could destroy it. So England for me was the land of books, libraries, believing in fairies – and the cinema. How I adored the cinema – and fortunately, we went a lot. It was so cheap. My favourites were cowboy films, because the cowboys were wild, and they galloped on fantastic horses. I never, never got out of my system desire to get on a horse and gallop across the prairie or alongside the sea. In due course, we had the opportunity to go for riding lessons in England, but it didn't give me what I craved for: speed, rough terrain, freedom; galloping as if the hounds of hell were after us. I had more fun galloping on my pretend horse through the shrubbery of parks and woodland.

But now, I was the age to have formal music lessons. The piano was my natural instrument – and we always had a piano, no matter how hard our circumstances. I don't mention music as a passion. It was like air to me. It was my oxygen. It never occurred to me to be without it.

My first music teacher was Miss Birch who lived with her brother, Mr Birch, in a neat suburban road of small, smart, well-cared-for houses just south of Ealing Common. This strange old-fashioned couple were old to me – but could have been middle-aged. Roly-poly round. He balding, she with tight curls round her head. She delighted in my desire to learn as fast as possible. The fact that I had a good ear and learned by heart meant that I skipped along through piece after piece. I had a delightful first book, with pictures – and lots of the titles to do with magic and fairies and goblin dances – thus guaranteed to fascinate me and help me to interpret the music. I remember her nodding and her curls bouncing as she said, 'Good, good, my dear! You're getting along like a house on fire!' I thought, that was a most unusual and strange compliment, though I always knew what she meant.

My brother learned from her as well – or perhaps from her brother. For Indra played the violin. We had our lessons one after the other. The lessons ended at half-past six in the evening. At quarter to seven until seven o'clock was the radio crime thriller series, with the racing music known as The Devil's Gallop and the announcer saying: 'DICK BARTON Special Agent' and his companions, Snowy and Jock. As soon as our music lesson was over, Indra and I raced down the road to catch the trolley bus back to Ealing Broadway, then chased each other down our road to our flat just in time for that thrilling opening theme.

At this point I should describe the Speakmans.

Bill and Edith Speakman were our landlords. But they were more than landlords. They were friends. My mother had been Cambridge with Bill's sister, Barbara, who died of TB. My mother became extremely close friends with Edith – a great pink-cheeked, strapping, no nonsense woman who looked more like a farmer's wife than a city landlady; who never wore lipstick and whose hair was forever drawn back in a pony-tail (until Bill died, when she chopped it all off, wore make-up and bought an MG sports car!). She had large white bare legs and always wore white ankle socks, even through the most bitter winter, when her legs would turn purple. But they were utterly loyal and good friends. My mother knew that whatever need we had for food, money or shelter, she would get it from them. Although they were the landlords for their various properties in that road which were quite rundown, they were honest and unexploitative. Their rents were cheap. It meant poor people at least had accommodation. Whenever we came to England, we stayed in one of their flats.

Bill believed himself to be an undiscovered genius, and maybe he was. By the time I became aware of him, he was a virtual recluse. People said that this was due to shellshock in the war. He had become agoraphobic – the fear of going out – and his world was encapsulated within the two shabby rooms of their flat and the long hall between the front door and the lavatory at the back. It was in this hall, in front of the row of gas metres, that he practised and taught the art of fencing. Many times, I would come home to see, through the frosted glass of the front door, his helmeted figure, with white protective chest pad and gloved hands holding out his long thin rapier, elegantly stretching out into an opening position with the soft unaggressive call 'En garde!'

Just to know Uncle Bill, as we called him, was to be educated. There seemed no limit to his knowledge. Even more mysteriously, he

was a Rosecrucian – one who belonged to a
Christian secret society (this society had been
founded in the seventeenth century and its
members studied ancient religious lores). It
was from Uncle Bill that I learned about vege-
tarianism, philosophy, violin playing, poetry
and painting. Having composed and written
and put his hand to many skills, he finally
turned to painting. But he was no amateur,
although self taught, it seems, at everything he
valued. He spent about two years just learning
how to draw bones of the human anatomy
then, when he finally felt he was ready to
commit something to canvas, he learned the
old classical skills of preparing a canvas. Just
as Leonardo da Vinci would have done, he
put on the first wash, allowed it to dry; put
on the second wash, dried it, then painstakingly applied those first strokes. He would
take months over a picture.

The biggest lesson I think I ultimately
learned from Uncle Bill was that each
individual sees the world uniquely. He painted

his environment: his street, gardens and neighbours. But what completely amazed me was that whereas I would have chosen dark colours – grey and brown and drab and depressing – Bill's pictures glowed with light and optimism. His colours were pastel and soft; blues and pinks and gentle yellows. He loved the fall of the lamp light, and the drizzle caught in its beam. He loved the reflections of wet pavements, and the flow of roofs against the sky.

He encouraged me to paint and draw and I was always rushing down to show him my efforts, though when I was six and seven, I was obsessed with painting fairies and cherubs.

He died some years back now, believing in his posthumous reputation. Alas, there's no sign of that yet – though, who knows?

One of their tenants in the basement flat was Mrs Gardener and her daughter, Ethel. Mrs Gardener was a lean, bony, hatchet-faced woman with a red nose, who looked

remarkably like the witch in The Wizard of
Oz. She tyrannized her daughter. Day in, day
out, we would hear her screaming at Ethel,
who often had red eyes and a red nose from
crying, even though she was a full-grown
woman. Ethel was her slave. Completely in
her mother's power. How I sorrowed for her,
and one day wrote a poem:

There was an old woman, who always used
　　to shout.
I used to watch her daughter go running in
　　and out.
One day her daughter ran away, the old
　　woman couldn't find her.
She ran into the woods to play and left her
　　home behind her.

That winter was one of the coldest on
record. I remember it too because I
desperately wanted to be an angel in my
primary school nativity play. I wanted to wear
the white gauze gown, the silver headband

with the halo attached to it. But though I begged and pleaded with my teacher, she explained they needed my singing voice in the choir, so I had to make do with staying in my school uniform.

We went to Newcastle-under-Lyme for Christmas. I remember windows opaque with frost and icicles hanging from the tap. But nothing stopped us playing. We slid and sledged and had snowball fights; we went carol singing and I saw my first pantomime which I thought was magical beyond belief; and I tried to stay awake for Santa Claus but couldn't, but found a scooter at the bottom of my bed on Christmas morning which was my pride and joy.

Chapter 6

Enemies, Friends and Siblings

I DON'T REMEMBER FRIENDS of my own in Batala. My best friend was my mother and occasionally my brother, if he let me in. My father was such a busy man that he wasn't such a major presence, though I remember him teaching me to ride a bike as well as taking me for evening rides on the cross bar of his bicycle. I also seemed content with my own company.

My first best friend was in England. I went to St Saviour's Primary School in Ealing, and there I met Doreen. Where I was dark-skinned with dark brown hair and eyes and obviously Indian, she was fair as day, with sparkling blue eyes and the most incredible head of tight, golden curls. We were completely inseparable.

She lived with her mum, Aunty Blanche and cousin Wendy over a shop in the Broadway. Aunty Blanche had skin as white as a ghost, and very black, drawn-back hair and black pencilled eyebrows. She was prone to fits. Wendy was a redhead with very freckled skin – and could truly be described as spiteful. Perhaps she was jealous of Doreen and me being such good friends. She was always trying to tag along and, as she was a bit older, seemed to delight in getting us to do things which could get us into trouble – like playing 'chicken' across the railway line. Nor was she averse to a touch of blackmail which mostly amounted to: 'I'll tell your mother of you.'

We roamed the streets of our neighbour-hood quite freely. I don't remember anyone expressing anxiety or warning us about dangers. My life then consisted of school, play, parks, music lessons, the library, streets, overgrown back gardens and the fish and chip shop on the corner. In school playgrounds we played endless skipping games and ball games, nearly all of them to an accompaniment of chanted rhymes. After school, we played cowboys and Indians, and hide-and-seek; we invented games in the park and looked out for menacing girl gangs. We picked up stray dogs, even if they weren't strays, and took them nobly to the police station. We went swimming often, in those freezing, shuddery, over-crowded swimming pools. There were three pools: the cheapest for sixpence, the less cheap for ninepence – and the most expensive for a shilling. Sometimes, just to have a quieter swim, we would pay the extra money, but not very often. In the autumn, we went conkering!

On 4th September 1947, my mother gave birth to her fourth child, a girl. She wrote to us – Indra and I had been sent away to a farm at this time – and said she was calling the baby Rosemary. I was incredulous. Why Rosemary? She had never mentioned calling her by that name, and as far as I was concerned, it had no glamour whatsoever! 'Why not Margaret?' I wrote back. The princesses Elizabeth and Margaret had the status of today's pop stars, though remembering all the famous stars of the time, I would probably have accepted Rita or Bette or Marlene. But Rosemary! It made no sense. So I refused to call her Rosemary, turning it neatly into Romie, which is what she has been called ever since.

Later, my mother admitted that she didn't know why she called her Rosemary. She had been considering all those literary names like Romola, Cicily, Dorothy (or Dorothea). She said a rather severe nurse asked her straight away what name should be put on the certificate, and my mother blurted out the first name that came into her head!

Don't get me wrong: I've nothing against

the name Rosemary. I just don't like it!

My brother and I had been sent to a farm in the country for missionary children who needed care, while my mother had her baby. At first we were perfectly happy because it was St Julian's Farm, where we had been before, just outside Horsham which was then deepest country. It was where my belief in fairies was at its strongest; so strong, that it almost hurt with the intensity. It's where I learned to sing the teasing song:

'Terry, you're barmy
You went to join the army,
You got knocked out
With a bottle of stout,
Terry, you're barmy!'

(Replace the name Terry for any child you were aiming it at.)

We always had good times there and this was the end of August so we joined in the harvesting from the hay carts pulled by huge

Shire horses, blackberrying, making jam, exploring, playing in the streams. It was the England I adored. They had lots of books, and it was there I discovered Cicely Mary Barker's Flower Fairies, and through her caught many more glimpses of fairies than I would otherwise have done. I also learned to love and adore Little Grey Rabbit.

Then, tragedy. My mother wasn't ready to have us home, and we had to be moved on. We were taken by car along the coast to St Leonards-on-Sea. There was a large family house, in which lived a mother, father and daughter. I don't remember their names, except the daughter's name was Vivian. Sorry to all the really nice Vivians who have this very nice name, but I hated this girl so much that I've never been able to separate the name from her.

She was a tyrant – as were her parents. Because of them, my brother started wetting his bed; we were constantly punished – and worst, worst of all, we had raw celery on the table at every meal time which we HAD to eat, or no dinner! It was fortunate that there also seemed to be an endless supply of bread, for that was the only way I got through the torture of each meal. I have managed, eventually, to quite like celery now – yes, even raw, but I have never got to like the name Vivian.

At last we were taken home. The whole ordeal probably didn't last more than a week or two, but I never forgot it. My brother and I raced down the road to see our new baby sister. Rosemary! I ask you!

While we were in England, a few weeks before my sister was born, India was handed over to the Indians. It was just before midnight on 14th August 1947 when Nehru, India's first Prime Minister, made his historic broadcast to the millions of Indians who all poured out into the streets waiting and listening, as he said, 'At the stroke of midnight when the world sleeps, India will awake to life and freedom.' So 15th August

1947 was brought in with such hope and ideals after one hundred and eighty-two years of British rule. It is strange to me that I have no recollection of that day. It's true we were England, but I suppose my mother was too involved in her pregnancy – my sister was barely a month away from born – and my brother and I were on holiday at St Julian's. I have no wonderful first-hand accounts of my own to mark this momentous day – for it was a momentous day – for India, and for England. This was the start of the break up of the British Empire; this was the 'jewel in the crown' which Winston Churchill had bitterly opposed giving up, more or less 'over my dead body'. Well, it didn't need to be over his dead body; the British electorate quite simply had elected a Labour Government after the war, and it was under a Labour Prime Minister, Clement Attlee, that India received her independence. But whatever the opposition, sadness, even bitterness, as the British had to watch the beginning of the end of their glittering Empire, they did it with pomp and ceremony and grace – as witnessed by Alan Campbell-Johnson, as usual at Earl Louis Mountbatten's side, the last Viceroy of India.

GOVERNMENT HOUSE,
NEW DELHI,
FRIDAY 15TH AUGUST 1947

I doubt whether it will be given to me to live through a more crowded or memorable day than this.

At 8.30 the trumpets and the scarlet-and-gold which had heralded in twenty Viceroys, summoned the State entrance of the newly-created Earl Mountbatten of Burma into the Durbar Hall, the first Governor-General of the free India. The strangeness of this great occasion lay not in its points of contrast with Mountbatten's earlier Viceregal installation, but in its essential similarity to the March ceremony. Now, of course, it was the function of an Indian Chief Justice, Dr

*Kania, to administer the oath to the
Governor-General, and for an Indian
Secretary of the Home Department to
officiate in swearing in the Ministers of the
new Dominion. Once again, the rich red-
velvet canopies were lit with hidden lights
above the golden thrones. The carpets were
a veritable field of the cloth of gold. Lady
Mountbatten in gold lamé herself adorned
the splendid scene.*

*The Mountbattens had only just taken
their seats on the throne when the whole
Durbar Hall resounded with the explosion
of one of the photographer's flash bulbs.
There was a momentary ripple of anxiety at
this realistic portrayal of a bomb. The
Mountbattens, with the full force of the
floodlights upon them, gave no outward
sign that they had either seen the flash or
heard the report. At the end of the
ceremony, the great bronze doors of the
Durbar Hall were opened and the link
between the old order and the new was*

proclaimed with the playing of 'God Save the King' followed by 'Jana Gana Mana'.

A few moments later and the whole distinctive company had dissolved, to be lost in the vast concourse massing round the Council House. No sooner had the Mountbattens on their State drive passed out of the main gates of Viceroy's – from now on Government – House and down the slope between the Government Secretariat buildings, than they were themselves engulfed and their landau almost lifted off the ground by the dense laughing throng.

Finally, I love Campbell-Johnson's postscript to his extraordinary account of that day:

Tonight I ran into the photographer ... He represents a paper of extreme left-wing persuasions, but this did not prevent him from shaking me by the hand and exclaiming, 'At last, after two hundred years, Britain has conquered India.'

No sooner was India given her independence – with all the regal pomp and ceremony of the British Raj – than all hell broke loose again. Neither Gandhi's pleas and fasting, nor his incredible journeys from one end of India to the other, begging or reason and restraint, seemed ultimately able to stem the ferocity of the communal violence which followed between Hindus and Muslims and Sikhs. For ten days, Amritsar along with Batala were put into Pakistan but, following a shriek of protest, were returned to India again.

On 30th January 1948, Gandhi was assassinated. That afternoon, crossing the gardens of Birla House to attend a prayer meeting, a man stepped forward. Apparently he was smiling as a friend – perhaps like Judas, when he stepped forward to meet Jesus with a kiss of betrayal – but then he pulled out a gun and shot Gandhi three times. Gandhi fell dying with the words 'My God! Ram, Ram!' Ram is the popular prince-hero and incarnation of Lord Vishnu. Panic swept round. The first

thought was that it was a Muslim assassin.
Mountbatten had been urgently summoned.
He arrived to find distraught, weeping
crowds, grief-stricken and panicked at the
thought of further mayhem. A voice cried out,
'Who killed him?' A man standing next to
Mountbatten answered, 'It was a Muslim,' to
which Mountbatten, with extreme presence of
mind and with a sixth sense, immediately
contradicted him. 'You fool, man, don't you
know it was a Hindu!' And thus, a murderous
riot was averted.

This description of Gandhi's death was
related over and over again, and there was no
denying the overwhelming grief into which
the country was plunged. Nehru wept as he
made his broadcast saying, 'The light has
gone out of our lives and darkness reigns
everywhere. I do not know what to tell you or
how to say it. Our beloved leader, Bapu
(father) as we called him, is no more.' But I
only heard these details later. It didn't mean
much to me as a six-year-old in London.

There must have been newspaper headlines. The one-legged ex-soldier on the corner of our road who sold newspapers, must have been shouting out, 'Gandhi assassinated!' But my mother heard the news from the milkman. Hearing his call in the street below, she had gone down from our first-floor flat to pay the bill. He up the steps carrying the milk, his face sad, and almost in tears he said, 'They've killed Gandhi! They've shot Gandhi!'

The British working people had grown to love Gandhi too. They knew that by wanting independence for India, he was not making them his enemy. He had already shown a great deal of sensitivity to the working classes of Britain – particularly those in the cotton mills and workshops of the North. When Ghandi began his campaign for Indian self-sufficiency, it meant he no longer wanted Britain to export her cotton to India, which Gandhi rightly perceived as being coals to Newcastle. India had cotton of her own which not only could be produced cheaper, but which should provide much needed revenue for Indian workers. But he also knew that by ostracizing the British cotton industry; he threatened the livelihood and the welfare of the British mill workers. On a visit to England, he went to Yorkshire to personally explain why he was in favour of this policy. When they understood, they supported him.

Mountbatten was right, Gandhi's assassin was a Hindu. Many Hindus thought that Gandhi had made too many concessions to the Muslims, an anger which culminated in this assassination – some would say martyrdom. Amazingly, by September, Jinnah too was dead – of cancer – within months of realizing his dream of creating Pakistan. His cancer had been kept a secret, and everyone wondered whether, if it had been known that Jinnah was dying, politicians could have hung on a little longer and saved India from having to divide into two. Was this karma?

By 1949 my father got a new posting to be Head of St Mary's Teacher Training College in

Poona, near Bombay. How my mother
skipped down the street in Ealing singing,
'Poona, Poona, Poona! Where the colonels
came from!' (for Poona had been a celebrated
British military cantonment). She was thrilled
to be going back to India and to show my
father his second daughter, now two years old
and who he still hadn't seen.

So back we went. Another wonderful
voyage to Bombay, then a train – the Deccan
Express, all the way to Poona. I went to St
Mary's School for Girls – a Church of
England Convent – and my brother went next
door to the boy's school, Bishops.

We lived in the Headmaster's bungalow over
the road and had a Goanese cook called
Lobo, and a squint-eyed bearer called
Garsum; he had a young girl wife, who hardly
seemed to know she had been born. I
remember she gave birth to a baby, and often
came and sat on our verandah. She would
prop this new baby up like a doll and then
not pay it any attention but sit and stare into

space. In due course, the baby, whose head was not yet firm, would roll over and bang its head on the hard stone. She would pick it up and prop it up all over again. I couldn't understand her neglect. Not long after, the baby died. I realize now, it was probably a girl. Girl babies are not welcome and the mother probably neglected her daughter as she herself had been neglected.

My main friends at St Mary's were my very best friend Maharukh, a Parsee; Gita, a Hindu; and Patsy, an Anglo-Indian Christian. A rather remote friend was a very reserved, beautiful Muslim girl called Nasreen – reputed to be a princess. Certainly she always looked more polished than us. I think she wore a change of fresh blue school uniform every day, and a servant used to come at lunch time with her own tiffin boxes. I rarely saw her smile and we never saw her after school.

In India, one of the first questions you can be asked is, 'What is your religion?' It isn't simply curiosity, it is also useful so that you can avoid unnecessary offence. One of the quickest things you learn is to respect all the different religions: that Hindus won't eat beef or Muslims pork; that Parsees leave their dead out to be eaten by vultures and Christians go to church on Sunday. You learn which hand to eat with and when to remove your shoes and all the different details pertaining to religion and custom.

Maharukh was beautiful. Her skin was as pale as a mango stone – and almost as hairy; I used to gaze in fascination at her arms of soft, golden down. Her hair was a richer, stronger version of the same and hung in two long straight plaits. Her eyes were light brown. If I say that she didn't look Indian, it's because she wasn't ethnically speaking. She was of Persian origins: that's where the Parsees came from hundreds of years ago, escaping persecution for being sun worshippers. How sad that India, which had always been able to accommodate and give refuge to every religion on earth, should have been divided by religion.

I went into Maharukh's household a lot; I saw her garlanded pictures of Zoroaster, and their small alcove set aside for prayers. I knew she wore a special white thread next to her skin; and I attended some sort of coming-of-age ceremony for her brother, Darius.

For some reason, although I was brought up a Christian, in a Christian environment – going to church sometimes twice a day, and Sunday School too; although I loved the bible stories – and knew the bible pretty well, I could never get round to believing in God. How strange that I found it easier to believe in fairies. Perhaps fairies were kinder.

The nuns at St Mary's enjoyed my love of music, especially Sister Dorothy Mary who taught me. I was making up my own tunes now, and she encouraged me to compose music for the girls to walk into assembly each morning. A visiting examiner from Trinity College of Music, London, came to stay with us, and that's when the seed was sown: the notion that one day I should go to England and study music. Certainly, it was pivotal in my mother's growing ambitions for our education. She was looking ahead, and wondering what was in store for me.

Chapter 7

Escapade on an elephant

IT IS THE CITIES THAT seem to make people cruel. Perhaps it is the breakdown of community; the desperation that has driven so many people there, seeking to escape starvation or the poverty of village life if the delicate balance of subsistence breaks down. But the cruelty, particularly towards animals, which I saw in Indian cities such as Bombay, I didn't see in the countryside. There, where I saw working animals like camels, buffaloes, elephants and horses, they seemed to be valued and cared for by their owners.

Of all the animals in India, I loved the
elephant the best. I still get a thrill out of
seeing this huge beast walking with such
casual, gentle, unaggressive elegance, and the
silence of its tread always astonishes me.

On the second anniversary of Indian independence, we were all visiting relatives in a
remote village. There was to be a procession
of celebration down the village street, and we
all turned out to watch. As my mother recalls,
one minute I was by her side, watching as
several elephants paraded down the street, all
painted and decorated and garlanded with
flowers, and their tusks all painted or
wrapped in silver and gold paper, and the
Mahouts holding up garlanded portraits of
Nehru and Gandhi, and the next minute I was
gone. There began a frantic search for me
among the crowds. Then suddenly, my brother
yelled, 'There she is!' And there I was, up on
the back of an elephant, holding the Gandhi
portrait. Well I remember longing to be up on
the elephant; the Mahout must have seen my

longing, for what I remember is being beckoned over and told to hold the elephant's trunk and stand on one of his great, huge feet. This I did. Then the elephant lifted his foot higher and higher, till the Mahout could grab me and haul me up. It took only a few seconds, and there I was, right on top, high above the crowds.

How proud I felt. What a moment it was for me. I stayed on his back all the way to a large field. Here, the elephants stopped and the pictures were removed. The elephants then dropped down onto their knees for the young lads of the village to bounce over their backs in a gymnastics display.

All afternoon, the elephants sat patiently, while they were jumped on and over and up and down. At last, at the end of the day, the Mahouts took the elephants down to the river where they got their reward. They went in and lolled over onto their sides, relishing the cool water and mud, while the Mahouts scrubbed their thick, wrinkled skin with stones. I joined in too, shrieking with pleasure every time an elephant sucked up water with its trunk and then snorted it out again.

Chapter 8

Now I am ten

M Y MOTHER WAS A restless person. She herself had talents and skills which had not been exercised for a long time. We didn't realize how close this was to being our final two years in India. It wasn't planned that way. We moved school yet again – this time because my mother had accepted a teaching job in Mussoorie, next door to the place where I was born.

We were to go to Woodstock School – as the school song puts it:

Woodstock! Known over all the land,
Woodstock! Sung of on every hand,
Woo-oodstock!

As I told them frankly when I revisited the place some forty years later, it was the single most miserable year of my entire school life. I hasten to say that for most children, Woodstock was an unforgettable paradise, the best possible school in the whole world.

It was then that I really appreciated what a spectacular place I had been born in. In a vast semi-circle, Landour and Mussoorie are enclosed by the mountains; the nearer ones with pines and deodar trees and rhododendrons and mountain oak, and the farther ones with the everlasting snows.

Woodstock was built on a wooded slope, with ramps which linked one bit to another. It was an American school with a large contingent of American children and a great variety of others, including British, Indian and Anglo-Indian.

I learned quite a bit about American life. I learned what a coke was; and loafers and jeans (which I craved, but of which my mother heartily disapproved). I learned about dollars, nickels and dimes, on top of what I had learned elsewhere about other currencies such as pounds, shillings and pence, rupees, annas and paise. I learned about dating and proms and graduation. I learned that whereas in St Mary's Poona, the question they asked was, 'What religion are you?' and in England a question could often be, 'Are you Oxford or Cambridge?' meaning which team did you support in the boat race, here in Woodstock they had to know whether you were Army, Navy or Air Force – and there was great rivalry between the forces. This was often exemplified in their songs. I learned all sorts of American nationalistic songs like 'When the Caissons Go Rolling Along', 'Anchors Away, My Boys!', 'Home on the Range' and 'Way Down in Dixie'. It taught me the potency of nationalism, and what rousing songs could do to feed it. As much as I hated the school and had not one single friend, never in my life had I felt such a desire to be American, just so that those songs could be my own.

Perhaps that's why I was so unhappy. Perhaps I encountered racism for the first time without understanding it. In betweeners weren't much regarded. It helped to be something – Indian, English, American, or even Canadian. Yes, my teacher was Canadian, and she was very tough on me. I was still considered to be quite bright, but my Maths was now really falling down, and she kept me in at break times to do extra work. But no matter how hard I tried, she never showed me any kindness. How I yearned to acquire an empty Venus pencil box, which she regularly handed out to pupils whom she considered worthy enough. Almost to the bitter end, it was never me, until in the holidays, tragedy struck. Her best friend, who had come over from Canada to visit, was killed in a car accident. My Canadian teacher was devastated. For some reason, it was my mother who became her main support and helped her through her dreadful grief and sense of guilt. Just before I left that school, she gave me a Venus pencil box.

We didn't have homework at Woodstock, and after school meant play, play, play. Play meant roaming the khudd, as we called the steep Himalayan hillside; it meant exploring and rambling with pen knives to cut striplings to make bows and arrows or carve bark; it meant carrying whistles which my mother gave us in case we got lost. And our ears always burned with her dire warnings about knowing what was at the bottom of the khudd – for a Himalayan hillside could end in a precipice drop of thousands of feet. A traveller to Mussoorie in 1837 wrote: 'The steeps about Mussoorie are so very perpendicular in many places, that a person of the strongest nerve would scarcely be able to look over the edge of the narrow footpath into the khudd without a shudder.'

But I must have been lonely, too, a lot of the time because at first my brother was in boarding school. It was much more fun for me when he came out. I never had known the reason why, and had never discussed my unhappiness at Woodstock until we were grown up. Then I mentioned it in passing one day, and to my amazement, he said it had been his worst year too. He had been constantly beaten up and taunted. My brother could fight back though – he was considered to be a proficient boxer, but by the end of the year, my mother had decided to call it a day, and it was back to St Mary's in Poona for me, and back to Bishops for Indra.

In 1952 King George VI died and we had a day off school; in 1953 Stalin died and my mother said, 'Oh good!' Our Indian childhood was now almost at an end – that is for my little sister Romie, and me. I was eleven, rising twelve, and my mother's instinct to get me a full English education and proper music lessons was strong. My father had now left

the Teacher Training College and become a
civil servant in the Government of India as
one of the first Tourist Officers. There could
be postings abroad, to America or Britain or
France.

That was it. We were on another boat – this
time an Italian boat which had started in
Australia and was crammed with Australians
heading for Britain in time for the Coronation
of Queen Elizabeth II, which was imminent.
My brother was left in Bishops to complete
his O Levels – the examinations we took those
days, which have now been replaced by
GCSEs – and would follow us later.

It was another voyage of sheer delight. It
was the ship's pool that drew me like a
magnet from dawn until beyond dusk. The
depth of the pool was from the deck to below
the water line – so it was very, very deep. I
liked to take a life belt, climb down the metal
ladder to the very bottom, then as they let in
the fresh sea water to fill the pool, I would
bob up and up with it like a little cork. Then I

swam and swam and swam all day and every
day. I can remember a scene as if out of a
Joseph Conrad short story, when I was still
swimming at dusk, and the ship's lights came
on over the pool. Gradually, as the black night
fell, you couldn't see beyond the barricade of
light. We were entering a harbour – probably
Port Said or Aden. Suddenly, I became aware
of dozens and dozens of eyes all round the
pool, watching me. Then I realized the ship
had docked, and all the porters and sellers
from the shore had come on board and were
staring at this funny frog-like creature
swimming around under the ship's lights.

So now this was England to stay, not to
visit. The England of the Fifties. Having
always lived in dingy one- or two-roomed
flats whenever we were in England, my
mother was now able to acquire a little
terraced house on the outskirts of Ealing, and
I went to a proper posh Girls High School,
where we had very strict uniform and very

strict rules and very high expectations put on us.

I cannot criticize the school – after all, it put up with me, and it recognized my musical abilities. My music mistress put forward for an exhibition to the Junior Section of Trinity College of Music, which meant that throughout the term, all my Saturdays were spent having a thorough and wonderful musical education: there was choir, orchestra, composition, piano and violin, and I came under the influence of the amazing Gladys Puttick who had pioneered music education for children. I wish I could have had that every day. At school, I was quite naughty, rebellious and very neglectful of any of the studies I wasn't interested in. I stood on my hands through needlework classes, and roamed round under the desks though French and often sat on the punishment bench though Maths. I felt constrained. I was bursting inside – bursting to do nothing but music and drama. Those were my great loves, and anything else, to me, seemed useless. We were always being told we had to have 'a standby' in case our extravagant ambitions fell through. So we must have our O Levels and A Levels and go to university etc. etc. But I was always rash and dramatic about everything. I just about got five O Levels, then left, even though I wasn't quite sixteen. 'Music,' I said, 'is all I want to do.' And when my form teacher told me what A Levels I would be taking, I said stoutly, 'Oh no I'm not'. Where other girls wept on their last day at school, I cheered. There is a photograph of me on my last day on the steps of the school and I'm leaping for joy. Today I would have fared worse. Today I wouldn't have been able to go to Music College without Maths O Level and two or three A Levels. It is considered that you can't possibly be musical without those! Huh! Even so, I wouldn't have been able to go without at least five O Levels, so I do have my Headmistress to thank, who, instead of throwing me out, which she must have been tempted to do, sat me down and told me that the reality was, if I didn't get my O Levels I wouldn't be able to study music as I so craved to do. So I worked – for the first time – and got what I needed. Nowadays, if I had failed, what would I have done? No doubt dropped out and joined the travellers and gone back to college in my middle age! Or just disappeared for ever down the plug hole.

Chapter 9

Childhood's end

SOMETIMES I FEEL THAT notions of heaven and hell and reincarnation are really all contained within one lifetime. Am I the same person as the child in Batala, the schoolgirl in Ealing and the music student in London? Was that the same me working on music programmes in the BBC; me, a mother of two living in Gloucestershire; me, a writer of children's books?

I married a blond blue-eyed man of mixed English, Irish and Scottish descent, and now I see my children, with no discernable Indian

blood in their veins, yet strongly aware of
their Indian heritage – and proud of it. They,
too, have names which reflect their mixed
blood: my daughter is Indra Helen Gavin; my
son, Rohan Robert Gavin. They have been to
India and know their Indian relatives. They
know that they are not just the sum of their
own parts, but of many, many parts which
extend across the globe. They will no more be
able to be simply categorized by race or creed
than I was. They are grown up now – but I
adored every minute of their childhood.

I loved my own childhood; I loved being a
child and I loved other children – mostly –
except Vivian! I liked what children
experienced and the way a fresh world was
opening up for them anew. I liked the idea of
being trapped in childhood – like Peter Pan. I
loved the fantasy world of children – the
fairies and witches and demons and ghosts.
Gradually, I stopped believing in fairies – but
never stopped loving the English countryside
which they inhabited. I still get a thrill from

seeing a gnarled tree or a deep hollow, or a
shady dell dark blue with bluebells; or a
stream, a bank, a valley or a line of bills. I
never stopped loving the sea. For all that, I
was – emotionally – a free spirit of India, and
even though I seem to have acquired my
melancholy here in England, England feeds
me as much as India did. To survive in
England, I had to find that inner world and to
allow my love of music and books to carry
me through. I am truly a child of both
countries and both cultures, and could not
deny either of them.

My life has been like one of Bill Speakman's
canvasses. It has had several coatings, it has
stood and weathered and dried. Painstakingly,
the picture has gradually been painted in, but
there are gaps – all the things I still want to
do in my life have yet to be painted in; all
those ambitions I had as a child: to go to
Tibet, drive in the Monte Carlo Rally, sail up
the Amazon, visit Petra, the rose-red city, and

go deep-sea diving in the Red Sea – all these things I want to add to my canvas. Today, I galloped on a horse along a beach through the waves lapping the shore. It is something I have wanted to do ever since I was a child. I have painted it in.

A BRIEF HISTORY OF INDIAN INDEPENDENCE

1929 Jawajarlal Nehru becomes president of the Indian National Congress.

1930-33 Three Round Table Conferences are held in London to discuss Indian independence. Gandhi attended the second, but the Indian National Congress boycotted the others.

1934 Muhummad Ali Jinnah becomes leader of the Muslim League, dedicated to Indian independence.

1936 George V dies; Edward VIII abdicates and George VI becomes king.

1939 Outbreak of the Second World War. Thousands of Indians fight with the British forces.

1942   The 'Quit India' Movement is launched in London: a free India will fight alongside the British but an unfree India will fight the British. In the same year, Sir Stafford Cripps, Labour MP, visits India to negotiate with Nehru and other leaders. The talks fail; Nehru and 10,000 Nationalists are jailed.

1945   The Second World War ends.

1946   Rioting throughout India. The people demand independence from Britain. Gandhi fasts to protest against partition.

1947   Lord Mountbatten is appointed Viceroy of India, to manage the handover of British power. 14 August at midnight, India becomes independent, with Nehru as Prime Minister. Jinnah becomes governor-general of the new Pakistan.

1948   January: Gandhi is assassinated. September: Jinnah dies of cancer

GLOSSARY

ASHRAM a religious retreat or place of study, particularly for Hindus.

AYAH an Indian nanny or nurse.

BEARER a house servant.

BINDI a red mark worn by Indian women in the centre of their foreheads; the mark may have a variety of meanings eg. it may represent caste or whether a woman is married.

BRAHMA part of the Hindu trinity, comprising Brahma, Vishnu and Shiva. Brahma is the god of Creation and is often depicted with four heads and four arms.

CASTE all Hindus are born into one of four main castes, which range from the highest to the lowest in society; priests (brahmans) and warriors (kshatriyas) are high caste, peasant farmers (vaishyas) are lower down the scale, while the unskilled (sudras) are at the bottom.

CHAPATTI flat, unleavened bread.

CMS Church Missionary Society.

DANDY a conveyance rather like a sedan, carried on poles by two men.

DHOTI a long cotton tunic worn around the lower half of the body by ordinary Indians.

FAKIR an Indian holy man.

FAST a period of days where no food can be eaten.

GANGA or GANGES the sacred river of the Hindus which is said to flow from the toe of the god Vishnu. It flows south-east across northern India.

GULI DUNDA an Indian game played like rounders, but with a stick and wedged chip.

INDRA Lord of the Heavens.

KARMA the Hindu belief that your fate is pre-determined. This belief is also shared by Buddhists.

KHADI raw homespun cotton cloth.

KHUDD steep hillsides of the Himalayas.

MAHOUT an elephant keeper.

RAGA a series of selected musical notes.

RAJ represents British sovereignty of India prior to independence.

RAJAH an Indian king or prince.

RICKSHAW a form of transport pulled by a man either on foot, bicycle or moped.

SHIVA part of the Hindu trinity comprising Brahma, Vishnu and Shiva. Shiva is known as the Destroyer.

TONGA a light two-wheeled horse-drawn vehicle.

UNTOUCHABLES the very lowest in the caste system, whose work is considered so unfavourable that they are beyond physical contact with people of other castes.

URDU a language introduced by the Moguls and widely used in northern India. It is the official language of Pakistan.

VICEROY the governor representing the monarchy in India at the time of British rule.

VISHNU part of the Hindu trinity comprising Brahma, Vishnu and Shiva. Vishnu is known as the Preserver.

WALLAH a term used with a particular task to describe a worker. It is used in a similar way to postman, milkman etc.

INDEX

Index